Tommy Atkins' Letters

The History of the British Army Postal Service from 1795

Contents

Foreword

The criteria used to determine what Special Exhibitions shall be mounted will vary according to the interests and capabilities of the museums in question. In the case of the National Army Museum a deliberate attempt is being made to relate the themes of Special Exhibitions to activities in the wider World usually relating to an anniversary of one kind or another.

reader will find a good story told in a lively manner, while the specialist will particularly welcome the publication of material from the Museum's Collections.

Apart from being alert to the opportunities presented by events outside the Museum, the staff are also aware of the changes in the methods of funding museum activities and the present Government's policy of

Italian Prisoner of War Postcard sent by Lieutenant-Colonel Robert Marlan, Australian Army, to Mrs C Roe at Healey Hall, near Rochdale, from Camp N78 in Italy, 5 June 1942. The reverse of this card is reproduced on page 39. National Army Museum 8901-106-1.

The occasion of **Stamp World London 90** at Alexandra Palace will draw a large number of postal historians and philatelists to London, and so it seemed precisely the kind of event to which the National Army Museum staff could contribute by staging a Special Exhibition on the history of the Army Postal Services entitled **Tommy Atkins' Letters**. Peter Boyden, Head of the Department of Archives, Photographs, Film and Sound, has been the Project Organizer and is the author of this volume published to accompany the display. The interested general

encouraging self-help through the seeking of commercial sponsorship. This Special Exhibition is an excellent example of this kind of cooperation with financial sponsorship being made available by Messrs Argyll Etkin Ltd of New Bond Street, London WlR 9FB, the renowned Specialist Dealers in Postal History, enabling this Publication to do justice to its subject. A particular debt of gratitude is due to James Grimwood-Taylor, who introduced the idea of this Special Exhibition when it was put to him to Eric Etkin and Angus Parker, whose undiminished enthusiasm for the project is greatly valued.

In the preparation of this Special Exhibition Peter Boyden has received a great deal of assistance from other members of the Museum staff, including Dr Alan Guy, John Quiddington, Alastair Pether, Adrian Carlton, Rebecca Daly, Jenny Spencer-Smith, Sylvia Hopkins, Lesley Smurthwaite, Dr Linda Washington, Ian Jones, Julian Humphrys, Marion Harding, Dr Mark Nicholls and Clare Wright.

Outside the Museum the National Postal Museum, Post Office Archives, Public Record Office and the staff of Argyll Etkin Ltd have provided every assistance in the research necessary for the preparation of the Exhibition and this Publication which accompanies it. The assistance given by the Defence Postal and Courier Services, co-ordinated by Captain Rod Small, is also gratefully acknowledged .

While the bulk of the items included in the Special Exhibition has been drawn from the Museum's own holdings, it has been necessary to supplement this with material from other sources. It is a great pleasure to acknowledge the generosity of the following individuals who have so kindly made available items for display: Frank Daniel, Ben Ferguson, John Firebrace, Alan Harfield, Honor McCulloch, Gerald Sattin, Elsie Smurthwaite and John Wilson. In addition Jean Farrugia and Douglas Fermer of the Post Office Archives and Tony Gammons of the National Postal Museum have readily agreed to the loan of material from their own archives for inclusion in the display.

Grateful thanks are also due to the Press Association Ltd, the Imperial War Museum, the Devonshire Regiment Museum, Exeter, and the Kent and Sharpshooters Yeomanry Museum for permission to reproduce and display photographs in their collections. Prints of illustrations credited to the Imperial War Museum are for sale on application to its Department of Photographs, Lambeth Road, London SEl 6HZ and its Visitors' Room is open to the public by appointment.

In conclusion, it is appropriate to stress that this Publication and indeed the Special Exhibition it accompanies should be seen as a tribute to all those soldiers who, often in the most difficult of conditions, have ensured that the letters were delivered - one of the most important morale boosters as any soldier will testify! Although the story which Peter Boyden tells starts in 1795, it should not be forgotten that the work continues in 1990 with soldiers under the command of Brigadier Neil Kelly, Director of Defence Postal and Courier Services maintaining the same very high traditions of service both to colleagues in particular and society in general.

Ian G Robertson
Director, National Army Museum
March 1990

People have been writing letters to each other since man first became literate. In the British Isles letter-writing did not become widespread until the second half of the sixteenth century and although a large percentage of the population were able to read and write, high postage costs restricted letter-writing to the higher echelons of society. For this reason, and the hazards to which documents are subjected over time, even letters written by officers on campaign are very rare before the eighteenth century while soldiers' letters are effectively unknown before 1750. Early letters that do survive are of exceptional rarity and interest, such as that written in 1650 by Colonel John Moore describing the defeat of Lord Inchiquin during Cromwell's campaign in Ireland, which has the words 'Hast Hast Hast' written on the address and emphasises the excitement of the disturbed times in which he lived.

Despite the creation in 1635 of a public postal service in Britain official interference with the mail made the sending of letters an uncertain and sometimes dangerous business before 1700, which is an additional reason for the scarcity of correspondence from before that date. There is some evidence to suggest that there was a special service for letters travelling to and from Marlborough's Army during the War of the Spanish Succession (1702-13) but it was not until 1743, during the War of the Austrian Succession, that the first distinctive postmark appeared on letters sent by British troops. The civilian authorities in the Low Countries sorted letters from the British Army separately, stamping them with a small circular stamp inscribed 'AB' for '*Armee Britannique*'. They also used a similar stamp, 'AA', for Austrian military mail. No other distinctive handstamps are known on British military mail until 1799, when two designs were used for letters passing to and from the Duke of York's Army in Holland.

As time passed the percentage of literate or semi-literate men serving in the ranks of the British Army slowly increased, despite the humble origins of many of those in its ranks. Parallel improvements in the postal service worldwide encouraged more officers and men than before to write letters to their relatives at home, even though the postage costs could be prohibitive. Before 1795 there was little difference in the eyes of the Post Office between a soldier serving overseas and any other British subject living abroad who corresponded with his homeland. However, in that year an Act of Parliament (35 Geo II cap 53) was passed which allowed seamen, non-commissioned officers and soldiers 'to send and receive letters by the post on their own private concerns' at a special low postage rate of one penny per letter, which was to be paid when the letter was posted. This piece of legislation was not designed to encourage correspondence between servicemen and their families (although it did have this effect) but rather to prevent the loss of revenue which resulted from soldiers being unable to pay the accumulated postage on readdressed letters when they ultimately caught up with them. Indeed, the year before the Act was passed, the Postmaster General had decided that in future only the original postage cost on redirected military and naval mail was to be charged on delivery. In order to qualify for the penny rate, the writer's name, rank, ship or unit had to be written on the outside of the letter, which was also to be signed by his commanding officer. These measures proved to be fairly effective in preventing the fraudulent use of this service by those not entitled to it. It also marked the beginning of the tradition, observed ever since, that British servicemen serving overseas should not have to pay high rates of postage in order to keep in touch with their loved ones.

Holland 1799

The first occasion upon which the penny rate was enjoyed by soldiers on campaign was in 1799 during the Duke of York's unsuccessful operations against the French in North Holland. The Duke's secretary wrote to the Postmaster General recommending

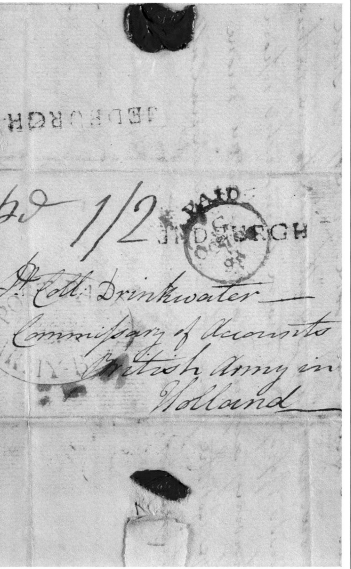

...from Jedburgh to the Army in Holland with the 'POST ... / ARMY BAG' handstamp, 22 Oct 1799. National Army ...um 8812-34

that 'a good and intelligent clerk should accompany the Army to manage the whole correspondence, to facilitate delivery, and to collect letters and *protect* the revenue'. The 'intelligent clerk' selected was Henry Darlot who, within a month of the secretary's letter reaching the General Post Office, found himself at Helder running the first British Army Post Office. The fact that he made an overall profit of £643.6s.6d during the two months that he was in Holland should not disguise the fact that he had to overcome such difficulties as sorting mail without any furniture to lay it out on, preventing officers from searching the bags for their own letters and not having any proper assistants. He also had to receive money for postage (1d for soldiers' letters and 6d each for officers') in any one of six different currencies, yet despite this he managed to give 'great satisfaction...to all parties on both sides of the water' and was allowed £1 per day 'for his services over and above his expences'. Unpaid letters from the Army in Holland were specially stamped with a black circular impression bearing a crown and the words 'ARMY BAG' above it; later a larger, oval stamp which bore the additional legend 'POST PAID' was used in red on prepaid letters.

The Peninsula and France 1809-18

The next occasion when large numbers of British troops were employed in Europe was during the Peninsular War, and on 31 October 1808 the penny concessionary rate was extended to the men serving in Spain and Portugal. Mail for the troops entered the war zone through the British Post Office in Lisbon and the army made its own arrangements for collecting and delivering it to individual soldiers. In April 1809, Lieutenant-General Sir Arthur Wellesley appointed Sergeant Richard Webb of the 3rd Foot Guards to act as 'Post-master with the Army' with an allowance of two shillings per day. With a corporal (later sergeant) assistant, he was based at Army Headquarters in Lisbon. However, in August 1811 Wellington reorganised the postal and courier services of his Army and made Major George Scovell, commander of the Corps of Mounted Guides, responsible for communications throughout his Army.

The British Packet Agent in Lisbon was responsible for the forwarding of the outgoing mail from the Army to England. In May 1812 commanding officers were instructed to send their men's letters with a list of them to either Scovell or Thomas Reynolds, the Packet Agent. The postage money on these letters (15 *reis*, equivalent to one penny) was remitted to Reynolds by the Deputy Paymaster General on instructions from Scovell. Later the same month the regulations were altered to allow soldiers stationed at Lisbon and Belem to take their letters and postage money direct to Reynolds, it being stated that the 'Post Office Sergeant at Lisbon or at Headquarters cannot receive soldiers' letters, and the money to pay the postage for them'. In December 1812 a strongly worded General Order complained of the 'slovenly manner' in which the orders for listing and sending the letters had been carried out. Between 24 and 31 October Reynolds had received 972 letters from 22 units, of which only 340 had been listed. Those from six units 'came loose and without lists, all mixed up', while those from another half dozen had arrived mixed up and two days ahead of their lists.

As his forces advanced across Spain towards France Wellington needed to shorten his lengthening supply lines which still stretched back to Lisbon. By November 1813 mail for the Army has ceased to travel overland from the Portuguese capital and was coming through the port of Pasajes, east of San Sebastian, where the Packet Agent,

Charles Sevright, was attempting with inadequate premises and staff to provide a postal service for the troops. In July 1814 an Army Post Office was opened in Bordeaux, where Sevright was now also based in more extensive accomodation than he had enjoyed at Pasajes and with the services of a civilian principal sorter (paid 12s per week) assisted by three non-commissioned officers or soldiers who were allowed six shillings per mail between them.

When Wellington assumed command of the Allied Armies on 5 April 1815 he had to create a command structure for his force from nothing. On 10 June Lieutenant-Colonel Sir George Scovell (as he had now become) was recalled to take over the communications of the Army and under him were two clerks in the Post Office at Headquarters, who were paid two shillings and one shilling and six pence per day. In addition, the civilian Director of Posts at Mons was paid 200 francs a month from 20 June for 'his trouble in arranging the correspondence from Head Quarters'. All mail to and from the Army had to pass through the Headquarters Post Office which after Waterloo moved from Brussels to Paris and by May 1816 to Cambrai. Soldiers' letters and the postage paid on them were transmitted successfully by the system used in the Peninsular and the mail was dispatched through the packet agent at Ostend, who by October 1816 (if not before) was Sevright.

Many letters from the Peninsula and France did not receive any postal markings until they reached the United Kingdom, although some letters from the Peninsula were stamped at Coimbra, Elvas and other places. On arrival at Falmouth letters which were not expected to travel to or through London were stamped 'LISBON / F', while those that reached the capital were marked by the Foreign Branch at the GPO in London.

Later Developments

Although wartime increases in postal rates at home were imposed in 1796, 1801, 1805 and 1812, the soldiers' penny rate remained unchanged. After the introduction of the Uniform Penny Post in 1840 (a reform that owed a great deal to the soldiers' rate) its use on inland letters effectively ended; but it continued to be a valuable concession to men serving overseas until 1898, when as in 1840, it was overtaken by the introduction of the Imperial Penny Postage. The concessionary rate was only available to men serving in the British Army. It was not extended to Britons who fought as soldiers in the Portuguese and Spanish civil wars of the 1820s and 1830s. However, men of the Royal Navy who became engaged in these campaigns were allowed to send their letters at the penny rate.

The situation in India and other territories administered by the Honourable East India Company was, however, more complex. Before 1840, soldiers' letters posted unpaid in India were charged three pence on delivery, one penny inland and two pence for sea postage, the latter going into the coffers of the Honourable East India Company which provided the ships. However, if the soldier prepaid the local Indian rate on his letter home it was only charged one penny on delivery. Between 1840 and 1855 different arrangements were in force so that letters posted unpaid in India and carried by packet boat were charged two pence on delivery,

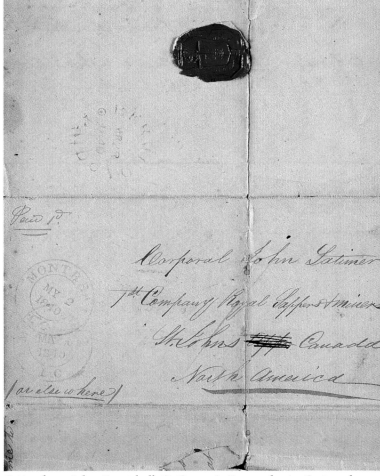

Letter from John Campbell, St George's Bermuda, to Corporal John Latimer in Canada, with 'BERMUDA / PAID' handstamp, 24 Mar 1840. National Army Museum 7205-2-17

one penny concessionary rate plus one penny fine. If these unpaid letters were carried on a private ship an extra two pence, which went to its captain, was collected from the recipient.

The Crimean War 1854-1856

The origins of the Crimean War lie in a squabble over jurisdiction of the Holy Places in Turkish-ruled Jerusalem which brought the Russians, as protectors of the Orthodox clergy, into conflict with the French, who championed the Roman Catholic cause. The Russians, intent on dominating Turkey and obtaining access to the Mediterranean from the Black Sea, began to occupy the Turks' Romanian provinces in July 1853. Turkey declared war in the following October, and on 28 March 1854 Britain and France did likewise in support of her.

Prior to the outbreak of the War letters passing between the United Kingdom and Constantinople were normally carried overland through France, transferring to French Packet Boats for the journey across the Mediterranean. The postage rate over this route was 1s 6d per half ounce, reduced to 11d on 3 April 1854, when the arrangements were changed so that the French only carried the letters between Constantinople and Malta from where British vessels took them on to Southampton. This arrangement did not last long, however, for on 18 May the Duke of Newcastle (Secretary of State for War) informed the Commander of the British Forces in the Crimea, General Lord Raglan, that an agreement had been reached whereby closed mails for the British Army would be carried six times a month by the French Post Office over the original route for the equivalent of three pence each for letters weighing less than a quarter of an ounce. The bags containing this mail were to be addressed to the 'Commander of the Forces in Turkey' and Newcastle suggested to Raglan that he should 'take such measures as may appear to you to be expedient, with a view to ensure to Her Majesty's Army under your command the full benefit of the arrangement in question'. Before Raglan was able to consider fully the implications of this plan

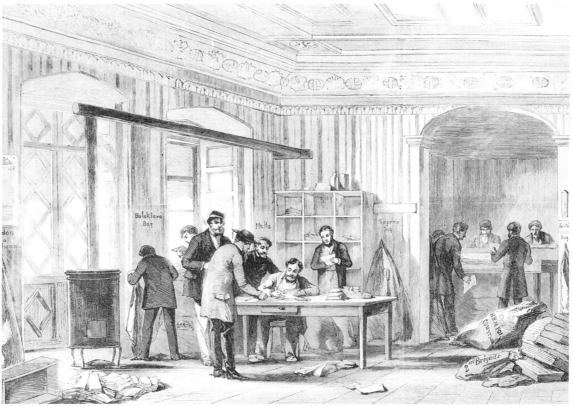

The British Army Post Office, Constantinople. From The Illustrated London News *19 Jan 1856. National Army Museum neg 72197*

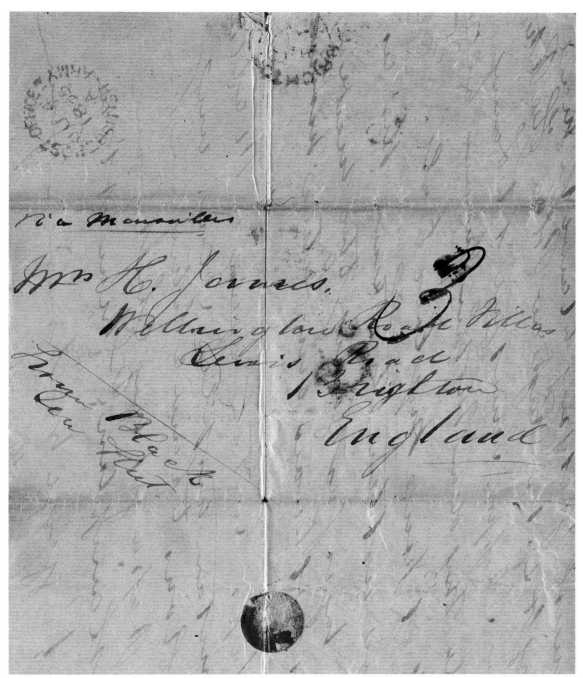

Letter from Henry James on S S 'Colombo' at Kerch, 27 May 1855 to Brighton. Sent at the 3d rate via Marseilles, with 'BRITISH ARMY / POST OFFICE / A' handstamp. National Army Museum 6901-46-2

the War Department was informed by the Post Office that 'with a view to relieving the Officers of H M's forces in Turkey from the irksome business of superintending the arrangement and distribution of the large mass of correspondence of which the mails between this country and the army are likely to be composed, the Postmaster General has determined upon dispatching an intelligent and experienced Officer of this Department to act as Army Postmaster'. The gentleman in question was Edward James Smith, who had acted in a similar capacity at Chobham Camp during the summer of 1853. Smith was

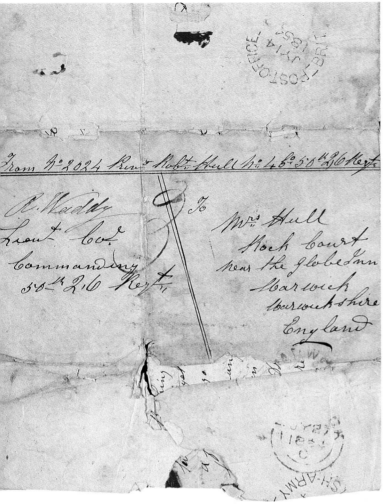

Soldier's Letter from Varna, 12 July 1854, prepared for posting at the penny concessionary rate but sent by the more reliable 3d service provided by the French. National Army Museum 7804-39-2

the postal service provided at the seat of war did not run as smoothly as had been hoped in London. The postal authorities complained to the War Department about the irregularities in the service caused by the late dispatch of mail from the Crimea to Constantinople so that it missed the sailing of the French packets. Mr Smith wrote to Rowland Hill from the Army Post Office at Balaclava on 23 November 1854 on this subject, stating that the difficulties had arisen from 'the want of forethought not only in the Naval but Military authorities'. In addition to contending with a shortage of steamers to carry the mail to Constantinople, the Postmaster also had difficulty in persuading the Army to provide transport to get the mail bags from the Post Office to the quayside. For these and other reasons, poor Smith was clearly operating under a great deal of pressure, as an unfortunate soldier discovered when he arrived rather late in the day with a bag of mail from the Light Division sent on the orders of its commander Major-General William Codrington. The Postmaster told the soldier to inform his General that although he was 'properly ready to devote the whole of the day time to the duties of the Post Office he requires at least the night to himself'. Complaints about this incident reached the War Department but there was not a great deal that could be done about it while the postal staff were employed by the Post Office and independent of the Commander of the Forces, a disadvantage which both Raglan and Newcastle registered forcibly to Hill in February 1855.

The irregularities of the service did not apparently discourage its use by both those serving in the Crimea and their correspondents at home. During 1855, over three quarters of a million letters were sent through France to the Army and Navy fighting the Russians, and one million two hundred thousand were sent back. Mail took about 36 hours to travel from Marseilles to London,

sent out alone, and it was intended that the military authorities would allow him 'one or two trustworthy persons' to assist him in his duties at Constantinople. Shortly afterwards, however, Thomas Angell was appointed Assistant Army Postmaster and later a second Assistant, Henry Mellersh, departed for the East. By January 1856, the establishment of the service had grown to three Assistant Postmasters, eight clerks and two local men who acted as interpreters. Two Postmasters and three clerks, assisted by two 'intelligent non-commissioned officers' were based in a Post Office in the Crimea.

Despite the presence of additional staff,

but the eight mails that reached Balaclava during May 1855 had taken between eleven and sixteen days to travel the complete distance from London. Although many soldiers opted to make use of the faster service across France, a few letters were still carried at the concessionary penny rate on naval vessels and transports, despite the even greater irregularity of this service. Outward mail to the Crimea had to be prepaid, but unstamped letters from the front were not charged double on delivery, a practice which was to be repeated in later campaigns.

On 30 May 1854 it had been decided that Smith should take with him to Constantinople £400 in 1d stamps and £100 in 6d ones (the latter for use on letters weighing between a quarter and a half an ounce). To cancel them, he had an oval stamp with a crown in the centre, a star on either side with three horizontal lines above and below, which was used between August 1854 and April 1855. Circular datestamps inscribed 'POST OFFICE BRITISH ARMY' were also used between June 1854 and September 1855. These had letters in the centre above the date line to indicate where they were used - 'A' at Constantinople, 'B' at Balaclava and later Army Headquarters and a reversed 'C' at Scutari Hospital. The crown 'killer' was replaced in May 1855 by the so-called 'OXO' stamp - an oval die in the centre of which was an asterisk flanked on either side by a letter O. The stamps on many letters from the Crimea were obliterated on arrival in London, having been backstamped with the 'POST OFFICE BRITISH ARMY' date stamps prior to dispatch.

After the initial difficulties had been resolved, the system of employing Post Office officials assisted by non-commissioned officers had worked fairly well. Less satisfactory was the Postmasters' independence of the Commander of the Forces, while the removal of the NCOs from their units caused problems for the military authorities. In addition, the subsistence allowances that the Postmasters received (Smith's was 21s per day) meant that the service had been expensive to run. It was to overcome these disadvantages that twenty years later the Secretary of State for War set up the committee whose recommendations resulted in the creation of the Army Post Office Corps.

Letter from Major George Mundy, 33rd Foot, Camp 'Allehdem' nine miles from Varna, with French 'ARMEE D'ORIENT / BAU A' handstamp, 22 June 1854. National Army Museum 8409-31-45

Until 1856 postal services for the Indian Army on campaign were provided by junior staff officers who were appointed by the Army to act as Postmasters. In the eyes of the Post Office these Postmasters were postal agents who fed their mail into the regular system at the closest available point. This system of self-help by the Army with the assistance of the Post Office came to a virtual end in 1856 when the Bombay Government, tasked with preparing for an expedition to Persia, asked the local Postmaster General to provide staff and equipment for a field post office.

The First Afghan War, 1838-42

At the beginning of November 1838, as the Army of the Indus completed the final preparations for its advance into Afghanistan, Captains Henry Havelock and W H Duncan were appointed Postmasters to the 1st and 2nd Divisions respectively. The former, a future hero of the Indian Mutiny, was replaced after five weeks by Captain William Sage who was paid a monthly salary of 150 rupees and equipped with a staff of eight *peons* (messengers) to act as postmen - one for each of the six brigades in the division and one each for headquarters and the Postmaster. A network of *daks* (relay runners) was established to convey the mail from the front to the base post offices at Ferozepore and Loodiana, the latter a pre-war office with extra staff.

As the Army advanced into Afghanistan the tribesmen became hostile and their attacks on the mail *daks* led at times to the severe disruption of the service, as well as heavy loss of life among these native letter-carriers. Havelock noted the receipt by one officer of an envelope 'thoroughly soaked in human gore', attached to which was a note written by a Deputy Postmaster which read: 'The sowar who carried this packet, was shot dead within two marches of Shah

Sooja's camp, and the envelope is stained with his blood.' In another incident, recorded by Sergeant-Major William Taylor of the 4th Light Dragoons, the postman was more successful in preserving his life and the mail that he carried. Attacked by two Baluchis, the postman was imprisoned in their hideout with his hands tied behind his back. His captors lay down to sleep, one of them using the letter bag as a pillow. Once he was sure that they were asleep the *dak* freed himself and going over to the man using the letter bag as his pillow 'placing his knees on his breast, cut his throat from ear to ear with a knife, which he took from the mountaineer's person, and made off with the bag'. Pursued by the dead man's accomplice for ten miles, he managed to reach camp, 'but in so weak and exhausted a state that nature was near sinking under the effort'.

Although the appointment of Army Postmasters was punctiliously recorded in Army Orders, in the early stages of the campaign there was a marked lack of central direction of the postal service and no scale of postal rates in use. Order was, however, shortly introduced into the operation of the service and, between May 1840 and January 1841, rectangular handstamps reading 'AFGHANISTAN / PAID' were in use at Kabul and, in 1842, two other, similar postmarks were introduced. In March 1840, letters took 20 days to travel the 1,715 miles from Sukkur to Calcutta. During the same month the post office at Sukkur received 341 rupees 3 annas in revenue, but cost 825 rupees 12 annas and 4 pies to run, a loss to the government of 484 rupees 9 annas. With deficits of this magnitude it is perhaps not surprising that in June 1841 the Governor General suggested that in order to recoup some of the heavy postal expenses incurred during the campaign the free transit of letters to the troops in Afghanistan should be withdrawn, although fortu-

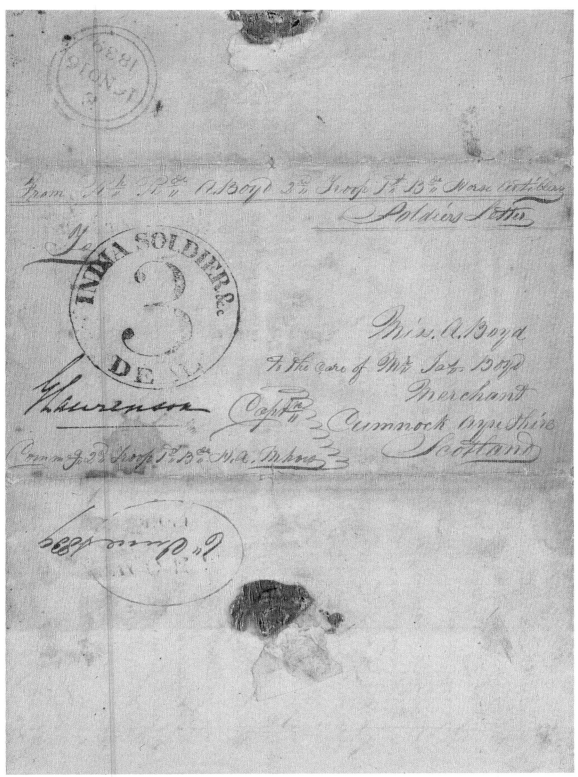

Soldier's Letter from Archibald Boyd, 2nd Troop 1st Brigade Bengal Horse Artillery, Mhow 3 June 1839. With 'INDIA SOLDIER & c / DEAL / 3[d]' handstamp. National Army Museum 5012-12

nately for the soldiers no action seems to have been taken on this proposal.

The First Afghan War was to be the last occasion in which large numbers of soldiers from India fought overseas without the benefit of a postal service provided by members of the Indian Post Office. While the system had functioned well, it was clear that operations involving thousands of men ranging over vast distances required the presence of properly trained postal staff in order to maintain communications with the outside world.

The Second Afghan War, 1878-81

While the need for experienced personnel to provide a postal service for the Army had been accepted by the authorities, there had been no contingency planning to cope with the sudden demand for facilities sufficient for a force of the size that was to be deployed in Afghanistan between 1878 and 1881. The need to staff the postal infrastructure required by the three Divisions that assembled late in 1878 placed a considerable strain on the Postal Department across India, while the demand for even more men to accompany the expedition sent to avenge the murder in September 1879 of Sir Louis Cavagnari, the British Resident at Kabul, had repercussions across the sub-continent. In addition to about 65,000 soldiers under arms it was also necessary to provide postal facilities for an even larger throng of camp followers, who were served by a network of civil post offices which operated alongside the military field post offices (hereafter referred to as FPOs). The need to cater for the postal needs of 150,000 people explains why, inevitably, the demand for skilled postal workers exceeded supply, and resulted in the employment of men who, although keen to receive the extra pay awarded to those in the field, understood little of the work.

The campaign began with a three-pronged invasion of Afghanistan by the Khyber and Kurram Valley Field Forces and the Kandahar Field Force. These operated independently, and each had Field Post Offices attached to them. Some FPOs initially used 'Camp of Exercise' datestamps and postmarks, but from May 1879 the military post offices were identified by numbers which appeared on their postmarks, the first numbered FPO postmarks in British history. These stamps were approximately 25mm in diameter and typically had three lines of text with the date in the centre, the number of the office beneath it and 'FIELD P.O.' inscribed above it. Of the three numbered FPOs known from this period, No 10 was situated on the Kurram Line, No 13 on the Khyber Line near Jalalabad and No 15 at Gandamak. During the operations which followed the renewal of hostilities in September 1879, FPOs were attached to each of the military forces and a horsed cart line was introduced between Peshawar and Jalalabad, later extended to Kabul. Fixed post offices were established in the south of Afghanistan for the use of the occupying force. By August 1880, five FPOs and 17 civil post offices had been established within Afghanistan on the Khyber Line, while Kandahar, the headquarters of the service for the north of the country, was the site of the only Head Post Office on Afghan soil. When the last of the troops left Afghanistan in 1881 the military postal service was also withdrawn and was not to be re-established until May 1919 when the Third Afghan War broke out.

Mail robberies, which had been a serious problem during the First Afghan War, recurred during the second conflict. During the course of 1878-79, there were 39 robberies in the whole of India, of which four took place in the area of the Afghan operations - near Thull, Kurram, Peiwar Kotal and in the Bolan Pass. The following year there were robberies at Kuch, Harnai, Dozan and three at Khalat-i-Ghilzai; and four more took place

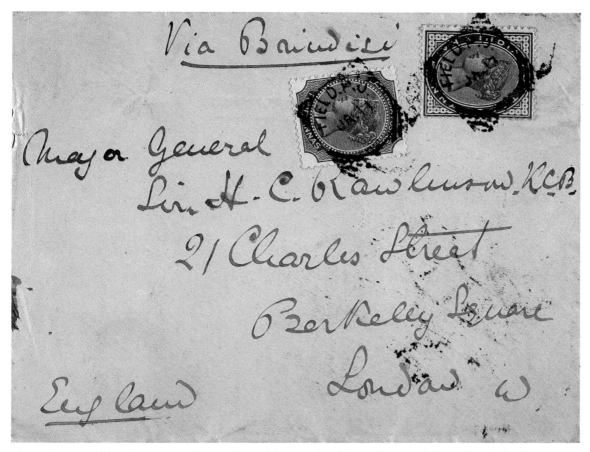

Envelope posted by Lieutenant Henry (later General Lord) Rawlinson while at the Delhi Camp of Exercise, 11 Jan 1886. National Army Museum 7212-6-397 to-402

in the area before the campaign ended. The large increase in the number of men in the North-West Frontier area had a considerable effect on the revenues received from the operation of the Bullock Train, Mail Cart and Parcel Van Passenger Service and the Punjab Military Van Dak. Receipts rose from a total of 903,868 rupees in 1878-79 to 1,344,738 rupees the following year, declining slightly to 1,337,099 rupees in 1880-81, and then slumping to a mere 540,816 rupees in 1881-82.

North-West Frontier Operations

While it was clearly necessary to have the services of competent postal staff during extended operations such as the Wars in Afghanistan, it was harder to justify their presence during smaller campaigns against recalcitrant frontier tribesmen. The 1880 edition of the *Regulations and Orders for the Army of the Bengal Presidency* included rules for the establishment of post offices in the field which linked the standard of the facility to the number of men engaged. Thus, for a force of less than 600 men, the commanding officer's staff officer was to distribute the letters without receiving any additional pay. Detachments numbering between 600 and 1200 men were to have a post office run by a sergeant, who was to receive staff pay and contingent allowances. Only when more than 1200 men were put into the field was a 'trained officer of the postal department' to be appointed, and even then the conveyance of the mails to and from camp remained the responsibility of the military authorities, who were also to supply the necessary equipage for the post office establishment.

Although from 1888 onwards the provision of Field Post Offices was a regular feature of large-scale operations on and beyond the North-West Frontier, for smaller expeditions the facilities provided followed the dictates of the regulations referred to above. During the punitive and road-building Lushai Expedition of 1889-90, for example, the invaders, who actually numbered over eleven hundred, made their own postal arrangements beyond the frontier, the letter bags being carried by the sepoys patrolling the road up to the base of operations. For the Chittagong Column which formed part of the Chin-Lushai Expedition of 1889-90, although the Post Office staff ran a FPO at Fort Lungleh, the carriage of mail was undertaken by armed soldiers under the orders of the General Officer Commanding. All incoming mail for members of the expedition was to be prepaid but they could choose whether or not to prepay the postage on their outgoing letters and packets - there was no outgoing parcels service from the FPOs, although the Base Offices at Gangaw and Demagiri provided a full range of services for those able to use them.

The official accounts of both the 1891 Black Mountain Expedition and the operations during the following year against the Isazai Clans on the Hazara Border contain separate reports on the postal aspects of

Mail day for the Seaforth Highlanders at Ali Musjid, during the Mohmand Expedition on the North-West Frontier of India, 1908. National Army Museum neg 67791

these campaigns. The former was compiled by William Van Someren, a future Officiating Postmaster General of the Bombay Presidency, who had first provided postal services in the field during the 2nd Afghan War. In his dispatch, Major-General W K Elles stated that 'The postal arrangements were complete in every respect, and to Mr W T Van Someren's care and attention in noting the changes in the disposition of troops the force is much indebted for the prompt delivery of their correspondence.' Van Someren's two-page report is a clear and methodical account of how he oversaw the provision of postal services for the troops, including details of the locations and opening and closing dates of his FPOs. The published page of extracts from Mr C G Dease's report on the postal operations during the Isazai Field Force betray a much less methodical approach to the provision of this important service. Instead of accompanying the troops, Dease apparently operated the service from the Indian side of the frontier at Oghi and had to rely on unofficial sources for news of the Army's movements. He failed to keep an adequate record of events during the campaign, and although his dispositions probably proved to be satisfactory, they must have lacked the crispness of Van Someren's organisation.

Until 1895 the FPOs attached to expeditions on the frontier used datestamps which were similar in design to those in use during the Second Afghan War. However, for the Waziristan Field Force of that year a new design was introduced, a smaller version of the type used extensively during both the World Wars. On this stamp the date was inscribed within a strip across the centre of the die and the letters 'F.P.O.' with the office number written within two parallel, curved

India General Service Medal 1854-95 with Chin Hills 1892-93 clasp awarded to Clerk T Kenny, Indian Army Postal Department. National Army Museum 8906-189

lines which ran round the circumference above and below the date.

As time passed, there was a tendency for the postal operations during these frontier expeditions to increase in size and complexity in line with their military and political scale. By 1914, the provision of a postal service for an Army in the field had developed a long way from the system in use during the First Afghan War, and the Indian Postal Service was well-placed to meet the challenges with which it would be faced during the First World War.

Africa, 1878-1898

The Birth of the Army Post Office Corps, 1877

The Crimean War was the last occasion when civilian postal staff were sent into the field with the British Army. In order to overcome the difficulties that had been encountered at that time and also to reduce costs(!) a Committee, chaired by Colonel Robert Biddulph, the Assistant Adjutant General, was established by the Secretary of State for War to consider 'the formation of a Corps for the performance of Postal Duties with an Army in the Field'. In its report, dated 28 February 1877, the Committee recommended that such a Corps should 'consist solely of men trained to the duties of the Post Office' and that the nucleus of it should be the members of the 49th Middlesex Rifle Volunteers. This unit had been formed on 19 February 1868. Its officers and men consisted of Post Office employees, who on account of the military training that they had received, constituted the ideal body of men to provide a postal service for an Army in the field.

The Committee recommended that during a campaign post offices should be established at the base of operations and at the Headquarters of each Corps, Division and Cavalry Brigade. The company of men required would be commanded by an Army Postmaster with the rank of Captain (irrespective of his Volunteer rank), with Assistant Postmasters (Lieutenants) at the base and with each Army Corps. The post offices attached to Divisions would be manned by a non-commissioned officer and two privates. The estimated annual cost of paying the 55 officers and men needed to provide a service for an Army Corps consisting of three Divisions and one Cavalry Brigade in the field would be £3,577 10s 8d, the men being paid 1s 6d per day.

Although after the publication of the Committee's report troops from Britain were engaged in fighting both the Zulus (1879) and the Boers (1880-81) the well-established colonial postal systems in southern Africa obviated the need for the embryonic Army Post Office Corps to take to the field, and it was not until 1882 that it began its active life.

The Zulu War, 1879

On 26 October 1878 Lieutenant-Colonel John North Crealock, Assistant Military Secretary to Lieutenant-General The Honourable Frederick Thesiger (shortly to become the 2nd Baron Chelmsford), wrote to the Colonial Secretary of Natal to suggest that as part of the preparations for 'a hostile advance over the Zulu border' (in the event of the Zulu king Cetewayo not bowing to British demands for a virtual protectorate over his realm) the colony's Postmaster General 'should be directed to wait upon him [Thesiger] to go into the question' of 'the postal requirements that would be requisite in such a military operation'. The meeting probably took place on 1 November when the contents of a memorandum that Thesiger had written previously were discussed. His intention was to invade Zululand at four points, with columns advancing from Lower Tugela Drift, Middledrift, Rorke's Drift and Utrecht, and he wished these lines of advance to be connected to the 'established Post stations...to which mail bags from the advancing columns would be sent by express riders or runners'. He requested the immediate establishment of a postal station at the Lower Tugela Drift so that information obtained by the Border Agent there could be speedily communicated to the Lieutenant-Governor at Pietermaritzburg.

The Postmaster General had little difficulty in arranging for the provision of native runners (in preference to horsemen who overtaxed their mounts) to extend the mail from Stranger, Grey Town, Helpmakar and Newcastle up to the Zulu border. He estimated that the service would cost about

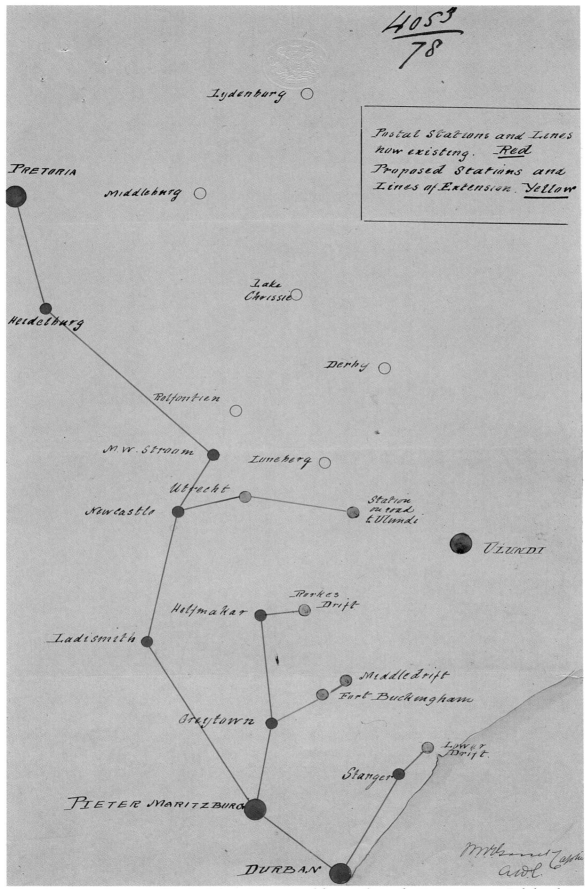

Map showing extensions of the postal service required for a military force operating in Zululand, *Nov 1878. National Army Museum 6807-386-10-16 (Part)*

£1,200 per annum and asked whether the charge was to be borne by Imperial or Colonial Governments. After some debate, it was decided that since the service was to be provided for the Army and would be of little benefit to the local inhabitants (of whom there were few) the Imperial Government should bear the cost of it. Before this matter had been settled Thesiger had followed-up his original memorandum with a further letters written by troops away from Durban and Pietermaritzburg should pass free, as had formerly been permitted within Cape Colony. This proposal was not accepted in its entirety, as the 1879 *Regulations for Field Forces in South Africa* stated that letters from the field to addresses within a Colony would be forwarded free of charge but that officers commanding troops should make arrangements for stamping letters sent elsewhere.

Envelope sent at the concessionary penny rate by John Herring, Natal Horse, signed by an officer in Bettington's Horse. The letter it contains is dated Pietermaritzburg 22 Jan 1879. National Army Museum 7612-84-7

paper of 5 November in which he requested that lateral communication between Rorke's Drift, Middledrift and Lower Tugela Drift should also be established making use of the Border Police posts along the river.

Colonel William Bellairs, Thesiger's Deputy Adjutant and Quarter Master General, who was responsible for working with the Postmaster General to establish the details of the service, gave some thought to the postal rates which would be used by the Army in Zululand. On 6 November 1878 he sent a letter to the Colonial Secretary in which he suggested that because of the difficulties of obtaining stamps in the field,

The same regulations also required the establishment of a post office in each column and made the officer commanding responsible for maintaining contact with his advanced post, to which the Post Office would deliver mail daily. Letters written during the campaign did not receive any postal or other marks until they were absorbed into the colonial postal system, when the postage stamps were obliterated by 'killers' and datestamps reading 'G.P.O. NATAL' were applied. Soldiers' letters to the United Kingdom continued to be charged at one penny, while the officers paid sixpence.

The Expedition to Egypt, 1882

When it was decided in 1882 to send a military force to Egypt to restore the Khedive and protect British interests in the Suez Canal, volunteers from the 24th Middlesex (Post Office) Rifle Volunteers (as the unit had now become) were called-for on 18 July to enlist in the Army Post Office Corps and serve in the campaign. The men had to agree to serve for six years, most of the time being spent on the reserve unless they were required for active service. They retained their positions in the Post Office, and when on campaign received their Post Office salary in addition to Army pay. This development provoked interesting responses among the Volunteer Movement generally which were recorded in the editorial columns of *The Volunteer Service Review*. In the issue dated 15 August 1882 the journal stated that there was 'far too much nonsense talked about volunteers embarking on foreign service' and that 'this proceeding has nothing to do with the Volunteer Force as such'. A month later, it stated that the men 'are actually regular soldiers at the present time, and will continue so until released from duty'. On 15 November the *Review* repudiated the view held in some quarters that the APOC men had done nothing to earn the campaign medals with which two of them were shortly to be presented by the Queen at a review of the troops returned from Egypt. The rest of the men received their medals on 15 January 1883, the *Review* pointing out that while they had not participated 'in the bayonet charge at Tel-el-Kebir' they had gone out to 'take any chances of war which might happen' and 'they dared the dangers of a climate ladened with ills for the present and evil influences for the future'.

On 8 August 1882, Captain George Sturgeon, Lieutenant Thomas Vial and their 43 men sailed for Egypt on *The British Prince*, reaching Alexandria on 21 August, where an Army Post Office was opened. On the 27th a Field Post Office was opened at Tel el Mahuta and from that date a postal service to and from the front was operated. Once the brief campaign ended in mid-September the APOC men assembled in Cairo with the exception of the detachment at Alexandria. On 7 October, the six men who remained to service the troops remaining in Cairo excepted, Sturgeon and his command left for home, receiving a tumultuous welcome in London on the 24th. During the course of the campaign, six Army Post Offices had been opened, numbers 1 and 2 at Alexandria, 3 at Port Said, and 4 at Ismailia, with numbers 5 and 6 accompanying the march of the 1st and 2nd Divisions respectively. These offices used circular date stamps inscribed 'BRITISH ARMY POST OFFICE EGYPT', and one cover is known with the impression of an oval 'killer' type handstamp inscribed 'B A / E'. In addition to making use of the facilities provided by the APOC the soldiers were also able to send via the Egyptian Post Office letters weighing up to 15 grams at a concessionary postage rate equivalent to one penny. Incoming letters addressed to non-commissioned officers and men could be sent at the penny rate, provided that they did not exceed half an ounce in weight. More than 7,000 troops were sent to Egypt from India and their postal needs were served by a separate service under the control of Mr J H Cornwall. He had with him a staff of fifteen who were equipped to man five FPOs, although only two of them, numbers 1 and 2, were actually opened. They were supplied with handstamps very similar to those used by the APOC, the killers having the letter 'B' in the centre and the datestamps reading 'FIELD FORCE P.O. EGYPT' and bearing the number of the FPO at which they were used .

The Expedition to Suakim, 1885

Sturgeon also commanded the APOC contingent which served on the Suakim Expedition in 1885, sailing with 20 men on 4 March to join the force being assembled on the Red Sea coast which was to advance inland to relieve General Charles Gordon at Khartoum. When the APOC contingent arrived at Suakim, a Base Post Office was opened in the Egyptian Civil Post Office building with a Branch Office on Quarantine Island. FPOs were attached to the Headquarters Camp and the 2nd Brigade, with extensive use being made of the local railway system to move the mail. Five date stamps and six killers of similar design to those issued in 1882 were dispatched from the GPO on 25 February for use by the APOC. The Army Postal Service closed on 30 May 1885 after which the Indian Field Post Office in Suakim served the remaining troops.

Upon their return home Sturgeon and his men were granted a month's leave to recuperate from the rigours of the campaign. The men of the APOC were not called upon to serve in the Sudan during its reconquest by the Anglo-Egyptian Army in 1896-98 as the postal service was provided by the Egyptian Post Office.

The postal service for the troops from the Indian sub-continent who participated in the Suakim Expedition was provided by fifteen men under the command of Mr F B O'Shea. They ran a Base Post Office at Suakim between March 1885 and May 1886 and a FPO located probably at Otao for seven months from 27 April 1885. Circular killers and datestamps were used, the latter were similar in design to those used during the Second Afghan War, with 'FIELD P.O.' inscribed above the date.

Field Post Office in the Sudan, c1898. National Army Museum neg 72200

Medals awarded to members of the Army Postal Service now in the Collection of the National Army Museum; top left: Volunteer Long Service and Good Conduct medal awarded to 2677 Sergeant J Carney, 24th Middlesex Volunteer Rifle Corps - the Post Office Rifles. Notification of the award was published in Army Orders *of Oct 1899. National Army Museum 9002-27*

Top right: Queen's South Africa Medal 1899-1902 with seven clasps awarded to 136 Sergeant H H Hinton, Army Post Office Corps. Hinton was still serving in South Africa in June 1901 when the roll of men entitled to receive the medal was compiled. National Army Museum 8906-35

Bottom: Decorations of Major H C Black, Royal Engineers Postal Section.
Hutcheson Campbell Black was appointed a Temporary Second Lieutenant on 26 July 1915 and reached the rank of Acting Captain on 12 Mar 1918. He arrived in Egypt on 16 Aug 1915 and in Jan 1918 was mentioned in Gen Sir Edmund Allenby's dispatch for distinguished service with the Egyptian Expeditionary Force. He relinquished his commission and was granted the rank of Major on 10 Sep 1919, and the award of his OBE was published in the London Gazette *on 12 Dec 1919. National Army Museum 8905-79*

The Boer War, 1899-1902

The War between Great Britain and the Boer republics, which lasted from 11 October 1899 until 31 May 1902, proved to be a serious test of the abilities of the British Army to wage War successfully against a civilised foe. The scale of the campaign, in particular the lengthy guerrilla war which covered thousands of square miles of country, necessitated the deployment of large numbers of troops, which in turn strained the resources of the support services, including the Army Post Office Corps.

The first detachment from the three officers and 98 men of the APOC mobilized on the outbreak of War to reach South Africa were Captain G W Treble, the Army Postmaster, 1 sergeant and six men who arrived on 29 October. Captain W Price, Lieutenant H F McClintock (Assistant Postmasters) and Sergeant-Major Yardley with eight sergeants and 52 men sailed on 21 October, with a further eight sergeants and 22 men following. On arrival they found some drummer boys valiantly trying to sort the mountain of mail for the Army that had accumulated in Cape Town. Base Offices were established there and at Pietermaritzburg to serve the force in Natal. Brigades and Divisions each had a Field Post Office staffed by a sergeant and three men who carried a stock of about £500 worth of stamps and postal orders. By the end of February 1900 there were 180,000 troops in South Africa, three-and-a-half times the number that the APOC establishment was intended to serve. Further drafts were sent out, but not all of the men were competent and despite being hand-picked for the job some of the NCOs in charge of the Field Post Offices did not prove to be very reliable.

Although the establishment of the APOC was raised in May 1901 to 396 all ranks, men from other units were liable to be drafted in to help out. Among them was Private Jack Dainty of the 10th Hussars who in June 1901 was sent to Army Post Office No 54 at Green Point Camp, two miles from Cape Town, where he was destined to remain until the civil authorities took over the service on 1 July 1902. He described the establishment in a letter to his mother as 'a large calvanized place half of which is for office work the other half our abode & very comfortable it is too - there is a sargeant in charge (a London P.O. man) then a corporal (a B'ham P.O. man) then myself, there are 3 other men to do the "rough" work - stamp - fetch the mail bags etc. etc. the grub is the same as the officers have - so you see I am not doing too badly.' [Spelling and punctuation as in the original.] Although Dainty worked in the post office, this did not necessarily guarantee the speedy delivery of his own mail and he often complained that he had not had a letter from his mother, even though in August 1901 he 'received seven newspapers in one day & a letter from Miss Andrew'. However, he enjoyed the work and hoped that a vacancy might allow his brother to join him there. Even when 'the fellow above' him was away and he was unable to leave the office it was 'no hardship as we don't open till 8.30 am, close for an hour at dinner time & close for good at 5.30 pm'. Although he clearly enjoyed his time in the post office he did not feel that the civil administration's wages, equivalent to £55 per annum at home, would tempt him (unlike some of his colleagues) to remain at the Cape.

Soldiers continued to pay the pre-war penny concessionary rate for their letters home from South Africa. The APOC had intended to sell British stamps for use on all soldiers' letters during the war but for political reasons was obliged to sell colonial issues for local correspondence, which considerably complicated their accounting procedures. Letters sent by troops on the march who were unable to obtain stamps were charged to the addressee at the rate which would have been prepaid, without any additional fine, as were unpaid letters from British prisoners-of-war. Back home, the Post Office had issued a notice on 7 November 1899 advising correspondents on how to address mail to soldiers serving in South Africa and advertising the concessionary postal rates of one penny per half-ounce for letters, a half-penny per 2 ounces for newspapers and 9d per pound for parcels, all of which helped to increase the quantity of mail that had to be handled at the front. In the period up to the end of September 1902 68.9 million letters and newspapers and 1.4 million parcels were delivered to the troops, of which 643,000 and 33,967 respectively were handled during the busiest week of the War. In addition, over two million pounds worth of postal orders were sold during the course of the campaign to men remitting money to their families at home.

At the end of the War Lieutenant-Colonel J Greer, Director of Military Postal Services, in compiling a list of APOC personnel recommended for awards, only included offi-

cers and NCOs in his return, since in his view 'a private has not much chance of distinguishing himself in the Post Office work'. Neither did the men normally have much opportunity to engage the enemy, although for Lieutenant P J Preece and his 18 men at Roodewal Station on 7 June 1900 this was not to be the case. They were part of a force of about 160 guarding 2,000 bags of mail, winter clothing for 20,000 men and other stores which had accumulated there for Lord Roberts' Army. 1,200 Boers commanded by General Christian De Wet attacked the station and after offering stiff resistance the defenders decided to surrender rather than be destroyed by their adversaries whose armament included five artillery pieces. Of the APOC men present, Private A Tuffin was killed, Pte J Gobel died of wounds, two were wounded and the other 15, including Lieutenant Preece, became prisoners-of-war. After it had been ransacked by the Boers the mail was burned, although some letters

Boers looting mail at Roodewal Railway Station, 7 June 1900. National Army Museum neg 17504

were later recovered and delivered. In addition to the letters and parcels the authorities also lost stamps and postal orders valued at £3,450 11s 4d on its way to restock six Field Post Offices and £1,651 14s 11d worth of stock belonging to FPOs 22, 23 and 35 in which the men at Roodewal were serving. As late as 1909 attempts were being made by British soldiers and their relatives to cash postal orders looted from the station and when De Wet's house was searched in 1914 over 3,000 unused British stamps, souvenirs of the attack, were found there.

In order to deal effectively with the Boer commandos during the guerrilla phase of the War, which commenced late in 1900, the Army was obliged to operate in much smaller units than had previously been the case. Brigades were broken up and infantry bat-

talions subdivided to garrison blockhouse lines or formed into *ad hoc* columns for field operations. These changes necessitated a reorganisation of the postal system which led to the establishment of Stationary Post Offices in place of the mobile Field Post Offices, augmented by five Travelling Post Offices running along the main railway routes in South Africa. The TPOs, in common with the FPOs, sold stamps and postal orders as well as delivering mail to soldiers based in the areas through which they passed. These organisational changes were also reflected in the cancellation stamps used by the APOC. Although datestamps which recorded a Post Office number continued to be used throughout the war, the establishment of the Stationary Post Offices gave rise to a series of datestamps which

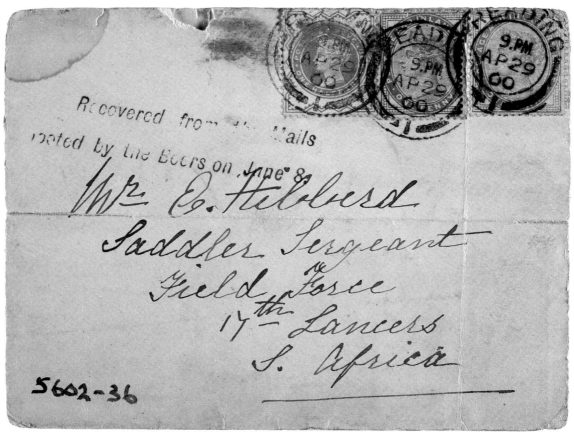

Envelope, posted in Reading 29 Apr 1900, marked with a cachet used by APO43 to the effect that it was among the mail looted by the Boers at Roodewal. Note that the date differs from that recorded in descriptions of the attack. National Army Museum 5602-36

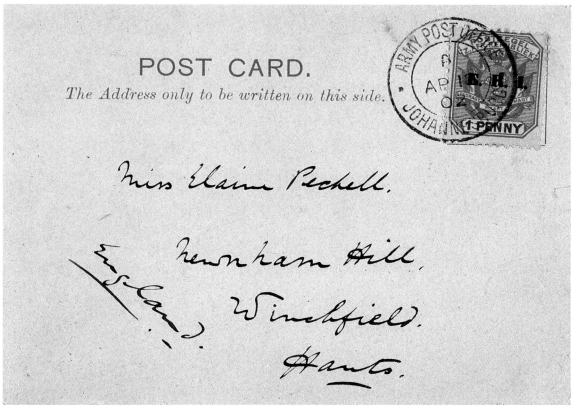

Anglo-Boer War Commemorative Post Card from Johannesburg to Winchfield, Hants, 12 Apr 1902, with Type III 'ARMY POST OFFICE / JOHANNESBURG' postmark. National Army Museum 6511-32-6

identified the location of the office. Two types of circular datestamp were made locally in Cape Colony, while octagonal stamps, again recording the location of the offices, were manufactured for the APOC in Natal.

The proliferation in the number of Army Post Offices and the variety of datestamps in use during the Boer War foreshadowed some of the developments which were to be seen more prominently in the First World War. A further facet of the War in South Africa which was to become of much greater significance after August 1914 was the censoring of letters. In order to prevent the passing of useful intelligence to the enemy, all letters sent to addresses in South Africa through the Army postal system were censored but there is also evidence from envelopes that private mail (in addition to dispatches from war correspondents) going overseas was censored on occasion. The Boers censored letters written by British prisoners-of-war: Major Frederick Evelegh of the Oxfordshire and Buckinghamshire Light Infantry in Pretoria noted in a letter to his son: 'the censor has cautioned me not to express my feelings so from now I must withhold my good as well as bad impressions - although the good predominate largely'.

The First World War 1914-1918

Organisation and Development

The Army Post Office Corps participated in the Army manoeuvres held in the United Kingdom between 1903 and the outbreak of the First World War, these exercises providing opportunities to test developing views about the level of postal facilities required by an Army in the field. The 1910-11 edition of the *Expeditionary Force War Establishments* provided for a Base Post Office manned by 85 all ranks under the command of a major who would also act as Deputy Director of Postal Services; Advanced Base Post Offices manned by six other ranks, one at each advanced base and two at each railhead; and Stationary Post Offices, operated by four other ranks, at each post on a Line of Communications. In September 1911, a conference of officers decided in favour of the preliminary sorting of outward mail in London with final sorting and distribution at the principal base. Under this scheme the Advanced Base Post Offices would have been replaced by a single establishment at the Advanced Base receiving mail from the Depot APOC at home. This thinking is reflected in the 1914 establishment of the Advanced Base PO which was increased to 32 men to include personnel for railhead duties.

On 28 February 1913, the Army Post Office Corps became a Special Reserve unit of the Royal Engineers and adopted the title Royal Engineers Postal Section which, by the time that War broke out in August 1914, had a strength of ten officers and 290 other ranks, sufficient for a force of six divisions. Mobilization began on 5 August and on the 12th, Captain J T Powney and Lieutenant T P Hobbins, each with one NCO and eight men, sailed to France to establish an Army Base PO and an Advanced Base PO respectively. The Army Base PO was set up in the Havre Club and dispatched its first mail on 17 August, receiving its first from home the following day. Reinforcements were constantly posted to it and on 6 October, as its War Diary records, 493 bags of mail were received from England, 589 dispatched to Field Post Offices, 126 were received from the field and 66 bags sent home. Already it was clear to Powney and his colleagues that the scale of postal operations during the current campaign was going to be much more extensive than it had been in South Africa. He noted that during an average December week (including Christmas mail) 789 bags of letters would have reached Cape Town from home. However, during the week ending 30 October 1914 2,087 bags had been received in France, while during the last seven days of November the level of postal work was 50.25% above what it had been in the same period of the preceding month. By 1917 the Army on the Western Front was sending home weekly 8,150,000 letters of the 8,926,831 from all the theatres of war.

In order to cope with this enormous quantity of mail, there had of necessity to be major changes in the organisation of the REPS. After difficulties had been experienced in undertaking large-scale sorting in France it was decided at the end of 1914 that it should be done more thoroughly at the Home Depot, which moved from Mount Pleasant to Regent's Park in 1915. From a staff of 30 on the outbreak of War its strength increased to 2,540 by the end of the conflict, most of them being women, and men who were medically unsuitable for military service. The expansion of the Army was accompanied by a parallel expansion in the number of Field Post Offices and Stationary Offices, the latter playing a growing part in handling the distribution of mail as the War progressed. The sorting of mail in London resulted in the renumbering, on 21 January 1915 of all the overseas Military Post Offices. For example, Army Post Office No 8, which arrived on the Western Front with 8th Infantry Brigade between 11 and 16 August 1914, was redesignated as Field Post Office No 8 on 21 January 1915.

Further changes were to follow during 1916, for early in that year British Military Intelligence discovered by studying captured German mail that it was possible to reconstruct the enemy order of battle from their postmarks. An examination of the British system where, for example, the FPO attached to 52nd (Lowland) Division Headquarters had the designation D.52 included on its handstamp, led to the decision to exchange the stamps used by FPOs on a three-monthly and later six-monthly basis in order to confuse the enemy. This practice began on 18 June 1916, shortly before the Somme offensive, and was continued until February 1919. To return to FPO 8, this unit used the stamps from FPO 44 between 18 June and 30 September 1916, from FPO 1 between 1 October 1916 and 31 January 1917 and from FPO 18 for the six months from 1 February 1917. For similar reasons there was from June 1916 a rotation in the numbers used by censors in marking letters.

Censorship

The censoring of letters had been introduced on the outbreak of the War, but it is clear that despite the network of censors and the fact that the REPS were forbidden to forward mail which was not signed by an officer and stamped 'PASSED BY CENSOR', many letters were being delivered in England that had not been censored. Men returning home on leave would often take with them letters from comrades to be posted in the United Kingdom, while correspondence sent by wounded men through the Red Cross also escaped examination. Many soldiers attempted to evade the censoring of their mail by sending it through the French or Belgian civil Post Offices, but these letters were intercepted and passed to the military authorities for censoring. It was clearly essential that in the event of a letter being intercepted by the enemy it should

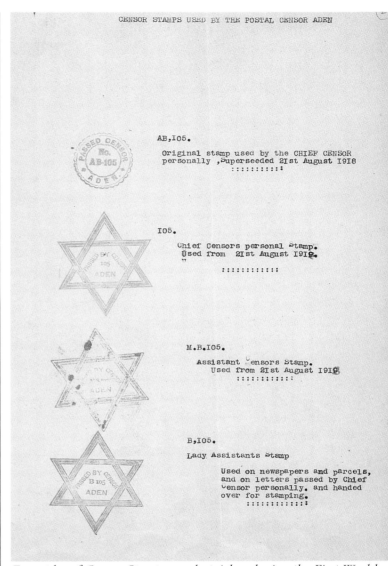

Examples of Censor Stamps used at Aden during the First World War. National Army Museum 8808-111 (Part)

not contain information about the location and or strength of particular units - and that it did not include copies of intelligence summaries, orders and other secret documents which some officers and men attempted to send home to their families. Equally dangerous, although for different reasons, was the habit of sending home 'souvenirs' such as 'shells, grenades, cartridges, fuzes and detonators' which was prohibited in a General Routine Order issued on 13 August 1915.

As the Army increased in size there was a

A Gas Sentry on the Western Front writing a Field Service Post Card, c1916. National Army Museum neg 24047

greater likelihood that news of impending operations, troop movements and other military information would leak into the hands of the enemy. In order to reinforce the need for 'keeping silence regarding all information which may be of use to the enemy' a pamphlet entitled *Censorship Orders and Regulations for Troops in the Field* was issued in November 1916. Among other matters, it restated the need to avoid giving away useful military information while on leave at home and listed nine subjects which were to be excluded from letters, including comments on the effects of hostile fire, the physical and moral condition of the troops and details of defensive works. It also gave details about the issue, custody and use of 'PASSED BY CENSOR' stamps and the arrangements for censoring mail both regimentally and at base. Two types of mail were not subject to censorship: Field Service Post Cards, provided that no unauthorised

additional information was written on them, and the so-called 'Green' Envelope. This was the 1915 successor to the 1914 'Red' Envelope, a blood-red form used for urgent letters which were exempted from censorship and other delays. The 'Green' Envelopes had on the front of them a declaration which was signed by the writer to the effect that the letter or letters it contained referred to private and family matters only. These envelopes were sometimes examined by Base Censors although they were exempted from censorship at a regimental level.

Postage Rates

On 28 August 1914 the troops were granted the concession of being able to send letters weighing less than four ounces free of postage to the United Kingdom and British Colonies. Letters weighing between four ounces and one pound were charged 4d until 24 July 1915 when each ounce over four was charged at one penny. Until free postage was granted Field Service Post Cards with a one penny stamp impression printed on them were sold by the REPS, but once they were sent free of postage they were distributed as stationery at unit level. Existing stocks of the 'stamped' cards were used up after 28 August and before the War ended at least seventeen different printings of the unstamped type were produced in various shapes and sizes, mostly in black ink on buff-coloured card. Many men wished to remit some of their pay to dependents at home and they were encouraged to do this by means of postal orders, which they could obtain free of poundage from Army Post Offices. In March 1916 an order was issued forbidding the sending of French banknotes through the post.

Persons at home wishing to correspond with friends and relations serving overseas were charged one penny per ounce for letters and one penny each for postcards. Printed papers could be sent for a charge of one halfpenny for every two ounces. Although registered letters were accepted, registered parcels could not be sent to members of the armed forces. These details, as well as instructions on how to address letters to members of the 'Expeditionary Forces' were included in a notice issued by the Post Office in January 1915.

The Indian Army Postal Service

Although the bulk of the REPS war effort was concentrated on the Western Front, they also provided full facilities for British troops serving in Gallipoli, Egypt, Palestine, Salonika, Ireland, Italy and Russia. In 1916, a REPS contingent was sent to East Africa equipped to establish a Base Post Office and six Field Post Offices, but none of them were opened as it was found that the Indian Army Postal Service in operation there was adequate. The REPS and South African Postal Corps personnel in the area were placed

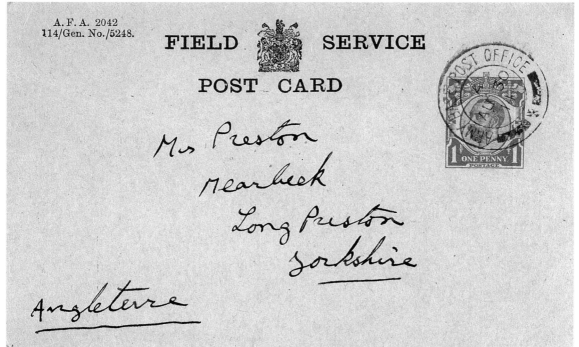

Field Service Post Card sent to his mother by Captain Thomas Preston, East Lancashire Regiment, while serving on the Western Front, 29 Aug 1914. With the handstamp of Army Base Post Office, then at Le Havre. National Army Museum 7704-58-14

under the commander of the Indian Postal Service. Not only did it provide a service for the troops in the area but its facilities were also used by the local civilian population, to the Base PO ('A') was moved, against British advice to Boulogne, from where it was able to deliver mail from Britain faster than the REPS could. Where troops from India fought

Sorting mail at Lala Baba, Gallipoli, 1915. Kent and Sharpshooters Yeomanry Museum, National Army Museum neg 72199

such an extent that during the course of the War over seven million unregistered pieces of mail were posted at Military Post Offices in East Africa.

The first Indian postal facilities to leave the sub-continent were the Base PO and 22 FPOs commanded by Lieutenant-Colonel Pilkington which arrived with two Corps at Marseilles on 26 September 1914. They were reinforced by three more FPOs in 1915 and

alongside British units they each normally operated their own postal systems. However, as the 'British' war effort in Mesopotamia was directed from India, no REPS personnel were present in that theatre and the postal service there was entirely the preserve of the Indian authorities. A Base Office and five FPOs left Bombay on 14 October 1914 and were based at Bahrain until War was declared with Turkey on the 30th. As the troops advanced up the Euphrates towards Baghdad, Field and Stationary Post Offices were established. The siege of Kut, which began in December 1915, posed problems for the Base Office at Basra. Although from February 1916 mail was dropped from the air into the town, and after their surrender General Townsend and his officers received some post from the Base, the bulk of the 4,000 bags at Basra had to be sent to London and India for onward transmission. During the renewed advance towards Baghdad in 1917 extensive use was made of both water and rail transport to carry the mail.

Postmarks

Most of the mail cancelled in the field by British and Indian Post Offices was stamped with circular datestamps. The typical REPS stamp was 25mm in diameter, with a layout derived from the types used during the Boer War. Between two concentric rings around the circumference were inscribed the words 'FIELD POST OFFICE' at the top and the office number at the bottom, with the date filling up the centre of the die. The Indian stamps were larger, 30 mm in diameter, and typically had the Post Office number in large figures with the date in small characters, inscribed horizontally across the centre of the die and 'F.P.O.' or 'BASE OFFICE' written between two parallel lines which curved round the top of the stamp. In addition to the date stamps, an enormous number of cachets were applied to letters by both postal and regimental authorities, with legends such as 'LOCATION UNCERTAIN / RETURN TO SENDER', 'UNABLE TO TRACE / A.P.O. S19' and 'FIELD SERVICE / POSTAGE FREE'. As with many other aspects of the Army Postal Service during the First World War, these cachets were developed from those used in South Africa.

Prisoner-of-War Christmas Postcard sent from Giessen Camp in Germany, with on the back a printed 'View from the Camp', 3 Dec 1917. National Army Museum 7609-35-18 (Part)

The Second World War 1939-1945

Inter-War Developments

The 11 November 1918 Armistice with Germany did not signal the end of hostilities for all units of the British Army. In Russia fighting against the Bolsheviks continued until October 1919 when the final elements of the North Russian Expeditionary Force left Murmansk. Their postal needs had been met by the REPS operating from Base Post Offices at Archangel and Murmansk which employed horse-drawn sleighs and Travelling Post Offices to distribute mail to the troops serving in the inhospitable Siberian climate. More fortunate from a climatic point of view were the 700 REPS personnel who served with the British Army of the Rhine. The poor state of the roads in post-war Germany obliged them to make use of Travelling Post Offices and aeroplanes to carry mail between BAOR Headquarters at Cologne and the French and Belgian Channel Ports. Both of these means of transport had been abandoned by the end of 1919, but between April 1924 and January 1926 a Forces Air Mail Service operated between Croydon and Cologne, parcels weighing up to two pounds being carried for two shillings. Outside Europe, REPS Volunteers also served with British troops in China between 1927 and 1940 and in Palestine during the revolt of 1936-37, when a total of eleven FPOs were open. In 1939 the REPS consisted of two officers and 44 other ranks based in Egypt to assist the Egyptian Post Office in processing mail for the British garrison, with a further fifteen officers and 250 other ranks (all Post Office employees) on the Supplementary Reserve.

The British Expeditionary Force 1939-40

The first REPS personnel began to move to France on 4 September 1939, being fol-

Postmarking letters at the Field Post Office at Chanzy Barracks, Le Mans, 26 Sep 1939. Imperial War Museum neg 035

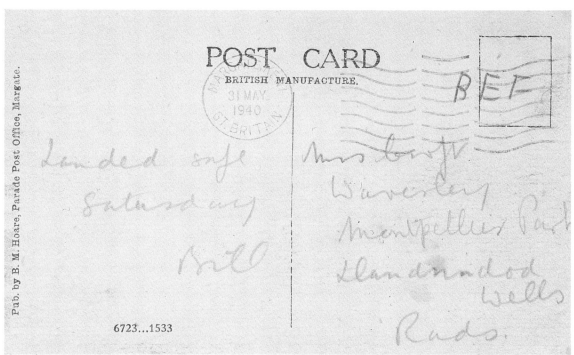

Post Card sent to his wife by William Croft, Royal Army Ordnance Corps, to report his safe return from Dunkirk. The 'BEF' endorsement ensured that such cards were sent post-free. National Army Museum 9002-51

lowed later in the month by the first of the fighting troops. In December the Folkestone - Boulogne route was opened and mail to and from the forward troops was channelled through Amiens. In addition to the land forces, the REPS also provided postal services for the RAF Advanced Air Striking Force and at the end of March 1940 twenty of its members were engaged on this duty. By that date there were 334 REPS staff serving with fighting units of the BEF and 241 on the Lines of Communications.

When the Germans began their invasion of Belgium on 10 May 1940 pre-arranged contingency plans were put into effect, but the speed at which the enemy advanced caused problems for the postal service. The Stationary Office at Boulogne was destroyed by bombing on 19 May and the staff on duty there killed. The following day the Germans reached the coast at Abbeville, thereby cutting off the Base Post Office at Le Harvre from the troops fighting north of it, for whom on 27 May the postal authorities had 26,000 bags

of undeliverable mail. When all non-operational troops were ordered to leave Boulogne, five to six thousand bags of mail were left behind under the guard of REPS personnel who managed to return with them to England shortly afterwards. The last mail sent home during this phase of the War in North-West Europe reached Dover on 29 May and 26 FPOs were lost during the fighting around Dunkirk. Upon arrival in Southern England the men evacuated from Dunkirk were given postcards to send to their relatives to inform them of their safe return home. Marked 'B.E.F.' in manuscript these cards were sent free of postage.

North Africa and Italy

The outbreak of War in September 1939 had little effect upon the postal service for the troops in Egypt, who continued to enjoy the concessionary rates allowed them by the local civilian postal authorities. However, the entry of Italy into the War in June 1940 severed direct air links with the United Kingdom and greatly increased the length of time it took for mail to travel between the two. In July 1940, REPS personnel were sent to Egypt and Palestine to establish a Base Post Office and two Lines of Communications units in readiness for operations against the Italians. In return for an annual payment of £1,000 the Egyptians allowed the British to run their own military postal service in the country, and the Stationary Post Offices at Alexandria and elsewhere were taken over and redesignated as Army Post Offices, identified by numbers prefixed with the letter 'S' (for stationary); similar establishments were set up later across North Africa as the Army advanced westwards. As a result of the October 1940 agreement with the Egyptian Post Office soldiers were obliged to have their letters marked with special 'Postage Prepaid' stamps in order to send them home at a concessionary rate. This rate was revised in May 1941 from 10 *mills* for a 20 gram letter to 10d for each 10 grams. Not until December 1943 were soldiers in Egypt able to send letters weighing less than two ounces free of postage. Cairo remained the centre of postal operations throughout the War in the Middle East and all mail passed through the city. By the end of the War in North Africa (May 1943) there were 53 Army Post Offices in the theatre serving the Lines of Communication areas and 35 British FPOs with the fighting troops. An additional 50 FPOs were operated in the theatre by the Indian, South African, New Zealand and other Armies.

With surface mail routes from North Africa to the United Kingdom redirected to the Cape or the USA runs, it was clear that the most expeditious means of getting mail to and from North Africa was by air, provided that its weight could be reduced to the minimum. Light-weight correspondence took two forms, Airletters and Airgraphs. The former were quarto-sized sheets of paper, which were folded into four and sealed along two edges. 160 of these weighed only one pound, and they were issued to troops at the rate of one per month. The principle of the Airgraph was that instead of manuscript letters, film copies of them were transported instead. The message and the name and address of the recipient were written on a special form which was recorded on reels of 16mm film. A roll of film weighing five and a half ounces contained up to 1,700 messages, photographic copies of which were produced in the country of destination and dispatched through the normal postal service. The photographic work was undertaken by Kodak and a postal charge of three pence was made for each message sent. By August 1941, there were photographic and reproduction facilities in London and Cairo, but by the end of the War these were available in places as far apart as Melbourne, Toronto and Fiji. The Airgraph traffic peaked in March 1943 when during one week over one and half million were dispatched from the UK. Thereafter, as additional aircraft capacity and supplies of Airletters became available, the number in use decreased, until the service was closed down on 31 July 1945, by which time over 330 million messages had been transmitted.

The force which invaded Sicily in 1943 sailed from North Africa and in consequence its postal service was controlled from Cairo, the first mail reaching the island from Tunisia on 13 July, just three days after the initial landings. After a fortnight, mail was being delivered by air to Sicily and the transit time for a letter from the UK was about six days. After the invasion of the Italian mainland postal services were at first disrupted by the delay in moving the British Army Post Office to Bari where it arrived nearly six weeks after the invasion began. On 14 October 1943, BAPO 15 moved from Salerno to Naples, which became the postal nerve-

Egyptian boys enveloping Airgraphs prior to dispatch to the troops in the Middle East, 13 Apr 1943. Imperial War Museum neg E23598

centre for the British Army in Italy. Drawing on the experiences they had gained in serving with the highly mobile Army in North Africa, the Army Postal Service was able to cope with the advance through Italy, and continued to provide a service to the remaining British troops until September 1946 when BAPO 15 in Naples was closed down.

Airletter written by Lieutenant-Colonel Harold Newman, Queen Victoria's Own Sappers and Miners, Bangalore, 31 July 1943, National Army Museum 7810-73-21 (Part)

North-West Europe 1944-45

In the planning for Operation OVER-LORD it was decided that letters would be delivered in Normandy on D+1, newspapers on D+4 and parcels on D+6, using air transport as soon as airstrips became available. The first REPS men to arrive in Normandy did so by parachute on the morning of 6 June and by the end of D Day the 40 postal staff in France had opened three Stationary Post Offices. By the end of the first week of the campaign their numbers had reached 200. The first mail for England had been dispatched on D+2 by Airborne Divisional Postal Unit and Beach Group Army Post Office, and after overcoming difficulties with marine transport the airlifting of mail began on 6 July. The rapid movement of the Allies across France and Belgium placed great strains on the postal service, whose railheads were rapidly left behind by the advancing troops. Nevertheless, they managed to deliver letters from the UK within an average time of two-and-a-half days from posting. From September 1944 aircraft flew into Brussels, as well as Normandy, in an attempt to improve the delivery time to forward units. Deteriorating weather in December 1944 resulted in a build up of more than 150,000 bags of Christmas mail in the UK which the Army Postal Service had to distribute to the Army in only two days, 23 and 24 December.

During the course of the War the REPS had undergone radical transformations in both its size and the way in which it operated. It was fortunate to have the services of men such as James Drew (1912-90), a Post Office employee and Special Reserve member of the REPS, who having been Deputy Assistant Director of Army Postal Services with the BEF served as Assistant Director of 21 Army Group and was responsible for planning the service that was to be provided after D Day. Having decided to make a career in the Army rather than the Post Office he attained the rank of Brigadier and became Director of Army Postal Services in 1959, and was in post in 1962 when the Forces Postal and Courier Service was created.

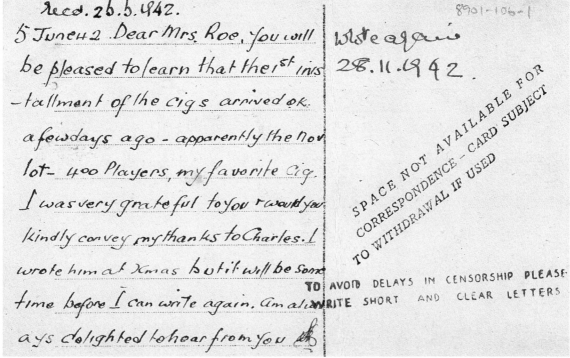

Italian Prisoner-of-War Postcard sent by Lieutenant-Colonel Robert Marlan, Australian Army, to Mrs C Roe at Healey Hall, near Rochdale, from Camp N78 in Italy, 5 June 1942. The address side of this card is illustrated on page 2. National Army Museum 8901-106-1

A soldier of 1st Battalion The Devonshire Regiment in Kenya reading a letter from home, 1953-55. From an album in The Devonshire Regiment Museum Exeter, National Army Museum neg 60354

The military and political shape of the Post-War World meant that Britain had to maintain a larger Army than had been the case after the First World War, with the British Army of the Rhine still in position at the time of writing. Developments in the Army resulted in a change in the status of the REPS from a reserve force of professional postmen to a permanent, regular force of professional soldiers and postmen.

After the defeat of Germany the BAPO in Brussels was closed and a British Zone Postal Depot opened at Herford in July 1946. This establishment was responsible for sorting all mail for BAOR - up to quarter of a million letters a day - until 1949, when the Home Postal Depot in London took over the basic division of the post by BAOR and later BFPO numbers. Travelling Post Offices were introduced between Hamburg and Herford, later running on other routes until they were withdrawn in the summer of 1949. The same year saw the introduction of a new system of Army addresses for BAOR, Middle East Land Forces (MELF) and British Troops Austria (BTA), whereby (for example) BAOR 33 was the address for troops based in Hanover, MELF 6 for Benghazi and BTA 1 for Vienna. In 1949 British Forces Post Office (BFPO) numbers were introduced and ultimately replaced the earlier system, BAOR 33 becoming BFPO 33 in May 1957, while MELF 6 was redesignated BFPO 55 in February 1955. Other British garrisons, not previously numbered, were given BFPO numbers, for example, Hong Kong, which became BFPO 1 in July 1949. This system has remained in use ever since, with numbers being added to the list to cover new garrisons and areas of conflict, including Aden, Cyprus and Northern Ireland.

Since the end of the Second World War, men from the Royal Engineers Postal Section and its successors have frequently been dispatched overseas with fighting troops. FPO 707 accompanied the first British troops to Korea in August 1950, while four other FPOs were deployed with the troops on Operation MUSKETEER, (the Suez operations,) during November-December 1956. These two theatres were assigned the respective BFPO numbers of 3 and 300. However, the first troops reaching Kenya in October 1952 to deal with the Mau Mau Emergency did so without FPOs and at first sent letters home with British stamps on them via the local civilian postal service. Six FPOs were later opened in Kenya and mail was handled at regimental level before being sent to Nairobi for transport to the UK. Because of the distances involved, the 1982 campaign in the Falkland Islands posed a major challenge to the men from 20 and 21 Postal and Courier Squadrons who provided the postal service for the men of the Task Force. They found it necessary to establish an FPO (BFPO 677) on Ascension Island as a staging post between Britain and the Falklands.

After the Argentinian surrender, on 14 June, an FPO was established at the civil post office at Port Stanley, which was used as the base for all incoming mail for the first week of the reoccupation. When the new airport at Mount Pleasant was completed in May 1985 a further FPO, BFPO 655, was established there.

On 30 June 1962 the Royal Engineers Postal and Courier Service became part of the Forces Postal and Courier Service and, operating from its Home Depot at Mill Hill, took over from the Post Office the postal service for Royal Navy vessels. Today, the Defence Postal and Courier Services are equipped to provide a similar service to that which their predecessors first provided in 1882 for the troops in Egypt. In a tent nine feet square two men with their equipment can supply a full range of postal facilities for troops on active service in the South Atlantic, on exercise in Germany, or indeed for visitors to a Special Exhibition at the National Army Museum!

Men of the Defence Postal and Courier Service helping to clear up the debris of the accomodation block at their Mill Hill Headquarters, damaged by an IRA bomb on 1 Aug 1988. Press Association Photograph 228623 (L)

Sources and Bibliography

This bibliography, which only contains sources which have been used in the preparation of this book, is divided into two sections. The first lists general works which contain further information about all or most of the chronological periods covered. The second part lists more detailed studies which cover narrower periods and or areas, which should be read in conjunction with the broader treatments listed in the first part.

The only complete history of British Army Postal Services in narrative form is Wells's study. Proud's volumes contain a great deal of detailed information about individual postmarks and the offices that used them, and in reproductions of official documents.

The following abbreviations are employed:

NAM - National Army Museum
POA - Post Office Archives
PRO - Public Record Office

1. General Works

R C Alcock & F C Holand, *The Postmarks of Great Britain and Ireland*, London (1940)

W G Stitt Dibden, *Postage Rates of H.M. Forces 1795-1899*, Postal History Society Special Series No 16 (1963)

R Lowe, *Encyclopaedia of British Empire Postage Stamps* Vols 1-3, London (1949-52)

E B Proud, *History of the Indian Army Postal Service*, 3 vols, Heathfield (nd)

E B Proud, *History of the British Army Postal Service*, 3vols, Heathfield (nd)

E Wells, *Mailshot, A history of the Forces Postal Service*, London (1987)

2. Archives and Detailed Studies

Beginnings

P B Boyden, 'Tommy Atkins' Letters: The Postal Service of Wellington's Army in the Peninsula and France 1809-1818' *Army Museum '83*, 1984, pp19-24

Crimea

Papers relating to the Postal Service in the Crimea
POA POST29/65, 70 & 71

Official Crimean Papers of Gen Sir William Codrington
NAM 6807-377 & -379

Crimean Papers of FM Lord Raglan
NAM 6807-281, -282 & -285

Africa

Papers relating to the formation of the Army Post Office Corps and the Egyptian Campaign 1882
POA POST30/449

Papers relating to the Egyptian Campaign 1882
POA POST29/363

Papers relating to the Suakim Expedition 1885
POA POST29/378

'Report of a Committee...to consider the formation of a Corps for the performance of Postal Duties with an Army in the Field' 1877
PRO WO33/30

Zulu War papers of General Lord Chelmsford
NAM 6807-386

Regulations for Field Forces in South Africa, Pietermaritzburg (1879)

The Volunteer Service Review, Vols. II & III, 1882-83

India

O A Chambers, *Report on the Lushai Expedition of 1888-89,* Simla (1889)

O A Chambers, *Report on the Chittagong Column, Chin-Lushai Expedition of 1889-90,* Simla (1893)

A E Hopkins, 'Post Offices of the Second Afghan War, 1879-80', offprint from *Bulletin of the Postal History Society* No 102 (1959)

A E Hopkins, 'Post Offices of the Second Afghan War, 1878-80: some recent discoveries', offprint from *Bulletin of the Postal History Society* No 110 (1960)

W Hough, *A Narrative of the March and Operations of the Army of the Indus...,* London (1841)

A H Mason, *Expedition against the Isazai Clans on the Hazara Border...in 1892,* Simla (1892)

D R Martin, *Further Postal History of the Second Afghan War 1878-81...A review in the light of contemporary records,* Postal History Society Special Series No 12 (1961)

D R Martin, *The Postal History of the First Afghan War 1838-1842,* Postal History Society Special Series No 18 (1964)

A H Mason, *Expedition against the Hasanzai and Akazai Tribes of the Black Mountains...in 1891,* Simla (1894)

Regulations and Orders for the Army of the Bengal Presidency, Calcutta (1880)

W Taylor, *Scenes and Adventures in Afghanistan,* London (1842)

W T Van Someren, 'A few remarks on past and hints for future postal operations in the field' *Journal of the United Service Institution of India* Vol. XIII, 1884 pp199-206

D S Virk, 'Indian Post Offices on War Service 1774-1913' in D S Virk, *Army Post Offices and Philately (A collection of articles).* India, 56 APO (1980), pp48-81

Boer War

Papers relating to postal services during the South African War
POA POST29/682, 693, 709

'Proceedings of the Army Post Office Corps in South Africa 1899-1902' by Major W Price
POA POST56/2

'Report on Military Postal Service' Jul 1900
PRO WO108/257

Recommendations for awards to APOC personnel 1902
PRO WO108/175

Letters of Private Jack Dainty, 1901-02
NAM 6807-425

Papers of Lt-Col F J Evelegh, 1891-1901
NAM 7807-57

A G M Batten, *The Roodewal Incident 7th June, 1900,* Bloemfontein (1981)

First World War

Directorate of Military Operations and Intelligence: Papers relating to Postal Services for an Expeditionary Force for France, 1905-11
PRO WO106/49

GHQ Troops Base Post Office War Diary Aug-Nov 1914
PRO WO95/144

Army Postal Services, General Bundle
POA POST30/4464

Special Postal Concession during 1914-1918 War
POA POST29/1240

B Gawthorne: 'Army Postal Services - British Expeditionary Force 1914-1919'
POA POST47/11

Censorship Orders and Regulations for Troops in the Field (Army Printing & Stationary Services), Nov 1916

F W Daniel, *The Field Censor System of The Armies of the British Empire 1914-1918, Unit Allocations I. War Office Based Types 1, 2, 3, 4 & 7*, Burnham on Crouch (1984)

Expeditionary Force War Establishments for 1910-1911, London (1911)

Extracts from General Routine Orders issued to the British Army in the Field Part II, General Headquarters (1 April 1916)

A Kennedy & G Crabb, *The Postal History of the British Army in World War I*, (1977)

War Establishments Part I. Expeditionary Force 1914, London (1914)

World War II

Papers relating to Cologne Air Mail 1924-26
POA POST 33/1087

Papers relating to Airgraphs
POA POST 33/6045 and POST102/5

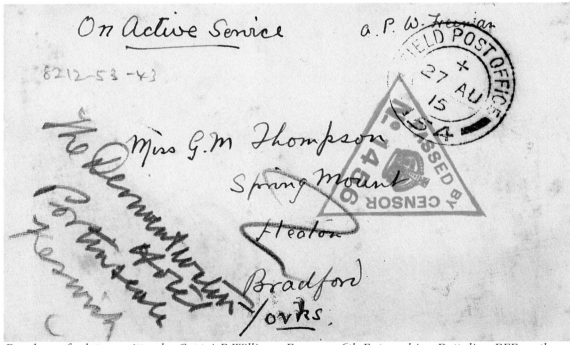

Envelope of a letter written by Capt A R Williams-Freeman, 6th Entrenching Battalion BEF on the Western Front, 23-26 Aug 1915, handstamped at FPO 54, attached to 54th Brigade, 18th Division. National Army Museum 8212-53-43

Index

Index

Decorations of 43 Private James Young, Army Post Office Corps. Young was born on 29 Dec 1858 and joined the Post Office in Oct 1873 as a Boy Sorter. A resident of Stockwell, he worked in the South East District Office. He reached the grade of Overseer in Apr 1897 and was retired on grounds of ill health in Sept 1908. He was awarded the Imperial Service Medal the following month.
He joined the 24th Middlesex Volunteer Rifle Corps - the Post Office Rifles in Feb 1881 and served in G Company. Young was among those who volunteered to serve in the Army Post Office Corps, and saw action in Egypt and Suakim, being mentioned in dispatches for the latter campaign. National Army Museum 9003-17